Heaven

According to Kids

"Heaven is all around us.
You can find Heaven at
church. Or on a boat."

-Evan, Age 7

"You get your very own puppy, and it never grows up! And your puppy has a pet elephant."

-Isabella, Age 7

"It's a place where you can eat anything you want, all the time, forever."

-Brennan, Age 9

"Happy!
And sunny!"

-Thomas, Age 8

"Everybody has a really cool car, like a monster truck, or a fire truck, or a race car. And you already know how to drive."

-Michael, Age 6

"Every morning you wake up and find out it's a snow day!"

-Jacob, Age 7

"When you go to Heaven, God carries your soul up in big buckets."

-Evan, Age 5

"Our cat went to Heaven, and now he gets to scratch everything without getting yelled at."

-Amelia, Age 5

"It's a place where anything can happen."

-Emma, Age 9

"Heaven is full of angels.
When they're not busy playing
games with their friends, they
keep watch over people on earth."
-Kendal, Age 8

"We can walk on the ceiling with God in Heaven."
—Dominick, Age 5

"If Heaven's in the sky, then there's no floor. So I guess people just float everywhere."

-Ava, Age 5

"There
are puppies and
kitties everywhere,
and kids playing
games."

-Joey, Age 5

"Playing follow the leader with Jesus on streets made of gold."

-Juliana, Age 7

"There's lots of birds,
and we get to play
trains all day!"
-Brennan, Age 3

Media Lab Books
For inquiries, call 646-838-6637

Copyright 2017 Topix Media Lab

Published by Topix Media Lab
14 Wall Street, Suite 4B
New York, NY 10005

Printed in China

ISBN-10: 1-942556-62-4
ISBN-13: 978-1-942556-62-6

CEO Tony Romando

Vice President of Brand Marketing Joy Bomba
Director of Finance Vandana Patel
Director of Sales and New Markets Tom Mifsud
Manufacturing Director Nancy Puskuldjian
Financial Analyst Matthew Quinn
Brand Marketing Assistant Taylor Hamilton

Editor-in-Chief Jeff Ashworth
Creative Director Steven Charny
Photo Director Dave Weiss
Managing Editor Courtney Kerrigan
Senior Editors Tim Baker, James Ellis

Content Editor Kaytie Norman
Content Designer Michelle Lock
Content Photo Editor Catherine Armanasco
Art Director Susan Dazzo
Associate Art Director Rebecca Stone
Assistant Managing Editor Holland Baker
Designer Danielle Santucci
Assistant Photo Editor Jessica Ariel Wendroff
Assistant Editors Trevor Courneen, Alicia Kort
Editorial Assistant Isabella Torchia

Co-Founders Bob Lee, Tony Romando

Illustrations by Le Thu from Sundog Studio

1C D17 1